The Baby Dilemma: How to Decide

Maree Stachel-Williamson

Copyright © 2014 Maree Stachel-Williamson

All rights reserved.

ISBN-13: 978-1505358643
ISBN-10: 1505358647

"Happiness is when what you think, what you say,
and what you do are in harmony."

Mahatma Gandhi

"With every experience, you alone are painting your own canvas, thought by thought, choice by choice."

Oprah Winfrey

CONTENTS

Acknowledgments

1	Prologue	Pg 3
2	Introduction	Pg 6
3	Debunking the myths of parenthood	Pg 12
4	Debunking the myths of being childfree	Pg 22
5	Positive goals vs negative goals	Pg 29
6	Exercises to help you decide - Parenthood or Childfree	Pg 32
7	Your results	Pg 66
8	Where to from here	Pg 69
9	References	Pg 71
10	About the author	Pg 74

ACKNOWLEDGMENTS

I am grateful to the many friends and colleagues with whom I have discussed this topic – Mum, Te Ruru, Broni McSweeney, Brian Carney, Marie Gant-Roxburgh, Leigh Hawthorne, Janaya Anisy, Joey Kingman, Ruby Myerscough-Nagy, Simon Grady, Pablo Moreno, Tom Molt & Daniela Karpe, Danille Grainger, Lynn Timpany, Tim Etheridge, Annie Milne, Miriam Lam, Kristine Ng, Irina Stachel and my beloved Jan.

An extra special thank you to Laurinda-Lee Grady and Lindsay Tallman for being my early guinea pigs for this books. Your input and feedback was fantastic!

Thanks to all of you for your honesty, insights and for helping me not only in the inspiration of this book but also for directly or indirectly helping me in my own journey.

1. PROLOGUE

From an early age I thought I'd have my own children. I helped raise my little brother who is 10 years younger than me. I've cared for over 30 children ranging from babies to young teenagers. I saved my favorite books from my childhood "for my own children" and still have them on my bookshelf as I am writing this book. I looked at boyfriends and wondered if they would make 'good dads'. I read books on child psychology and parenting and even kept a inspiring text book from University on raising children with special needs – just in case.

I feel very fortunate that I haven't been subjected to endless queries of 'when' or 'if' I am going to have children that I hear other women are bombarded with from friends and family. The only 'grandchildren speech' I've ever had from my mother was on her 48th birthday when she told me she didn't want to become a grandmother before the age of 50.

Every now and then, my friends and I have joked about who's going to be the next to have kids and people often ask if I have children. But I don't feel any pressure from them or from society.

When I hit my 30s, I suddenly noticed a new pressure from within myself about the decision. This was due to being close to the age I thought I would be when starting a family. And therefore, this is also when I began to ponder the decision seriously. To my frustration, the more I thought about it, the more conflicted I felt. Sometimes it felt obvious and positive to start trying to get pregnant (how exciting and fulfilling!) At other times, the idea of a child 24/7 in my life seemed ridiculous (how would I cope?) The ongoing discussion in my head and out-loud was both exhausting and confusing.

Not everyone experiences this confusion. For me, part of the dilemma came from knowing that I am great with kids and having many wonderful experiences already. I imagine all those beautiful feelings I've had as a child-carer are tenfold when they're your own. But when I've talked to parents, many of them say they love their children, but also find raising them a struggle. No-one seemed to like my question of whether they would choose to have children again if they could turn back the clock. Perhaps the question is challenging because they cannot turn back the clock and are already parents. Yet, I still have a choice. If you're reading this, I'm going to assume you still do too.

Eventually, the way I answered the question for myself (and with my husband) is as follows: I started by first addressing my fears and motherhood related issues and then considering the consequences of each option more rationally and from many different angles.

The more I looked at the issue, observed parents and non-parents alike and talked to people in both scenarios, the more I realized that there are actually heaps of people out there who end up getting stuck in this dilemma and not being able to reach a decision. It's for them and others like me for whom I have written this book.

2. INTRODUCTION

For thousands of years, women didn't get to choose whether to become a mother or not (and in many countries they still don't). If you didn't want a child you would have to run away to a nunnery, try to avoid sex or semen being released into your vagina, then basically cross your fingers and hope for the best. Condoms were originally in the control of men or even the law, and even if you could get your hands on them, religious beliefs often created a fear of hell if you used them. Thankfully, the introduction of diaphragms in the 1930s and then birth control pills in the 1960s heralded the modern age in which women suddenly had more control and choice over *when* or *if* they were to become a parent.

Some people will continue to have beliefs that clash with the idea of contraception in any form. I'm not going to be discussing the philosophies of right or wrong in this book. Instead, this book aims to help people who are fortunate enough to be living in a place and time when they have a choice. Not just women, but men and everyone in between also. Individuals as well as couples.

The 4 main types of people when it comes to parenthood

1. The millions who know for certain they want to raise a family ... or not. And who simply go ahead and do what they need to do to make their goal a reality.

2. Those who, through recklessness or statistical improbability of contraceptive failure, have an 'accidental' pregnancy.

3. People who due to their culture, generation or beliefs don't feel they have a choice. Parenthood in these cases is expected and a given.

4. The many who see good and bad points of either option and get stuck. They may like some aspects of raising a family but also don't feel they *'have to'*.

To be in this last situation is both a blessing and a curse because you realize that either way, the outcome of your decision will have a massive impact on your life. Often the fear of making the wrong decision leads to feelings of despair and confusion.

My husband and I understand the challenge of this decision because we belong in the fourth group. Funnily enough, my husband was the first partner with whom I could imagine raising a family and he says the same of me. Yet we each found ourselves unsure as to whether we actually wanted to become parents. We're both strongly independent, value our freedom, enjoy working flexible hours and are introverts needing peace, quiet and time alone in order to recharge our batteries after a day of people contact. Yet, we both love children and enjoy many aspects of being with them. On top of that, we can also imagine the joy of doing activities as a family – cooking, growing vegetables, singing and making music, story time and tucking our little ones into bed at night.

As we pondered the topic, we noticed others who were also asking themselves the same question. And like us, they also struggled with finding a way to be able to figure out how to make such a momentous decision.

Who this book is for

This book aims to help all those who get the luxury (or dilemma!) of choosing whether to have a child or not. It's for individuals and couples who need help to find their answer to this very important question - to address the topic of raising a child and becoming a parent and to be guided to think about the topic in new and creative ways that will help shed some light on the matter.

I don't intend to try to convince you to have children or to remain childfree (after all you're the one living your life). I'm just going to offer you some new insights and angles on the issues so you can explore the topic in what I hope feels like a neutral way.

How to best make use of this book and the exercises in it

If you don't have a partner, then just work through the exercises by yourself or with a friend if you prefer. If you have a partner and are unsure that they will be supportive during your exploration process, then you might like to do the exercises by yourself first, as this can become a heated topic due to differences of opinion. If, however, you are in a relationship in which you feel supported and know you can freely explore your thoughts and feelings, then I definitely recommend reading and doing the exercises together while continuing your discussion and sharing insights along the way.

This is the time to be brutally honest with yourself – if you want to make the best decision possible, then you need to give yourself time and space to consider and answer each exercise truthfully. Also, I expect many readers to reach their decision over a matter of days, weeks or even months. Therefore I recommend you write your ideas down so you can refer to them later. Some questions may also prompt you to do your own research – from other books (on parenting or living childfree for example) or by talking more to people in both situations.

And if you are reading this book as a teenager, or are in your twenties, your decision may be dependent on your current partner, job or age – this is also something for you to consider. What you decide as a 20-year-old may or may not be the same as a 35-year-old!

Explaining my chosen terminology

Throughout the book I use the terms 'have a child', 'raise a family' and 'become a parent' interchangeably. The reason for this is to address the variety of situations that my readers are in. Some hold the view that if they're going to choose to become parents, then they will have at least two children. Others are just considering the idea of one child. Many will be pondering the situation of getting pregnant, carrying it to full-term and giving birth. Others are considering the choices available via IVF, surrogacy or adoption. Some people reading this will be singles, others couples, some married, others not, some heterosexual, others in same sex or other relationship combinations. Therefore, make sure you don't get caught up in the terminology I use. Consider the situation and go through the exercises thinking about how it relates to you. If a particular exercise doesn't relate to you at all, then just move on to the next one.

You'll note that I also use the term childfree within this book rather than childless. I came across this term a few years ago and personally find it a much more positive word and more reflective of the situation (just like it makes more sense to say a biscuit is sugar-free rather than sugar-less). To call someone childless has a negative connotation and therefore I've chosen the other more positive wording. The reality is that both options work for many people (being a parent or not). One is not necessarily a better choice than the other.

About the rating system

I have included a self-assessment to help give you not just the insights that I hope you gain from each exercise, but also an overall evaluation of where you lie in the extent of your parenting desire. I have specifically chosen to only give you two options after each exercise – essentially forcing you to choose an extreme that reflects either a life as a parent or one childfree. Originally I included a middle neutral position, but from testing found that it didn't add anything for people who are essentially already struggling with the options. To rate yourself after each exercise, simply pick the answer which feels nearest to how you feel. I've worded them as extremes on purpose and it's okay if you don't feel as extreme as I've put it.

The benefit of the non-numerical rating system that I have used is that even if you skip an exercise or two because you don't find they relate to your situation, it will have no bearing on your outcome. You can complete as many or as few of the exercises as you wish – the rating system will still work. Of course, the more you complete and rate, the richer and thus more accurate your end assessment will be.

3. DEBUNKING THE MYTHS OF PARENTHOOD

There are many reasons that come to mind when people think about the benefits of having a child or children. While enticing in their promises, it can be useful to look a little closer at the truth that lies behind the assumptions and debunk some of the common beliefs that circulate about parenthood and having a family.

Note, I'm not saying that the following scenarios never happen – of course they can and when they do your life will be further enriched. However, relying on the following scenarios as solid reasons to have children may only cause extra grief if they do not materialize.

Parenthood myth 1: Having a child means I'll have someone to support and look after me when I'm old

We all know the scenes from the movies: the elderly parents are visited regularly by their adult children and the grandchildren for lunches on the weekend, their children also pop in for a chat during the week and call just to check in and make sure things are okay.

Sounds great, right? Well, we all know some families have this closeness – spending time together and providing emotional and practical support, and yet many don't. The reality is that the elderly often end up in rest homes and many complain that they feel forgotten by their family.

The idea of a family-based community built upon several generations in which members take care of each other is extremely attractive. Is this the type of culture you live in though? Even if it is, can you imagine telling your child they were brought into this world in order that you have company and someone to love you in your old age?

Even if you have raised your child with lots of love and they gladly love you back when you're old, the reality is that they might have to work full-time, raise their own family and they might live in a different city or even country than you. It might not be sensible to choose to become a parent if your sole reason is to have someone care for you in your old age.

In addition, coming from a culture in which family responsibility and expectations are high does not guarantee your children will look after you in old age any more either. In many rural areas around the world, the young are breaking with old traditions, moving to the cities away from extended family and building modern urban lifestyles for themselves which follows the Western trend of living in small nuclear family units.

Parenthood myth 2: Having a child will give my life meaning and purpose

This is an interesting argument because lets face it, it's true. By becoming a parent you are pretty much guaranteed a strong sense of meaning and purpose in your life. But seriously? No pressure, kid! If this is the reason for your child's existence, right from day one you've put an enormous pressure on them to fulfill your needs and that's an pretty unhealthy reason to bring a new life into existence.

While having a kid will definitely give your life a deep sense of purpose, it might be better to have a child because they are wanted for their own sake and as a parent you can then enjoy the feeling of purpose that comes as a result.

You can hopefully imagine the difficulty this 'reason for existence' would cause when a child starts becoming more independent, hanging out with their friends more than with you and eventually leaving home. Empty nest syndrome can be hard enough as it is without this extra heaviness of your life's meaning resting solely on your child.

On the other hand, some people have a sense from an early age that they want kids and that having a family is something that is ultra important to them and isn't a question of 'if'. It is as if 'family' *is* their life purpose. But those people don't end up having this dilemma of wondering in the first place and thus wouldn't be reading this book!

Parenthood myth 3: Having a child will be a good way to improve my marriage, to save my relationship or to make sure my partner stays with me

Sure you will have a new source of love and shared pride in the little miracle you've brought into the world and the love with your partner will gain a new depth. Nonetheless, the reality is that couples often report child raising as *the* most challenging thing in their life. Raising a child is hard work!

From sleepless nights, having less energy, a lot more to do and the challenge of finding time to spend alone as well as together as a couple, you are going to be challenged and stressed as a couple in ways you never have been before. If your relationship is already shaky, a baby is only going to shake it further. And what happens years down the track when your 'marriage glue' leaves home?

If you already question the solidity of your relationship, a good place to start is nurturing the bond you have with your partner and put time and energy into creating a strong, loving relationship that is more likely to last the distance regardless of whether you choose to have children or not. Otherwise you'll just be faced with the issue of a rocky relationship again in the future – although sometimes people find the distance has grown even more over the years because they put all their focus onto the child at the expense of their relationship.

Parenthood myth 4: Having a child will make me happy

Many studies looking at the effect parenthood has on happiness levels reach the conclusion that parenthood does not increase happiness and often lowers it. New research from Princeton University however paints a more complex picture.

Their findings show that there isn't a simple answer to the question of whether you will be happier as a parent or not. What the study revealed, is that out of the 1.8 million Americans followed, those who were parents reported higher highs and lower lows than non-parents on a daily basis. For example, the parents' self-reported happiness scores were 1.4% higher than the non-parents but they also reported 5% more anger, 6% more worry and 10% more stress.

Despite all the negative emotions felt by parents, studies often fail to pick up the many magical, emotional highs that parents experience and say make any stress 'worth it' – for instance, upon seeing their child smile at them or proudly showing off a new skill or running to greet them after some time apart.

I personally wonder if people who consciously decide to have children experience higher levels of happiness than those to whom parenthood accidentally happens. In that same way, I wonder if people who are childfree by choice are more likely to have higher levels of happiness than those who want children but are biologically unable to. To my knowledge, no-one has researched this yet.

What we do know is that even those who consciously choose to become parents can be shocked to discover the reality of parenting is much harder and less satisfying than what they expected.

Therefore, whether you personally will be more or less happy if you become a parent is pretty impossible to predict. You can look at statistics on levels of happiness according to your age, sex, marital status, income level and all the other factors that statistically have an impact on an average parent's happiness. But, you don't know what will happen in your life (and your child's life) down the track just as you can't foresee what a childfree future will hold for you.

Pinning your happiness on your child is also a huge responsibility for that child to carry. I've worked with several teenagers dealing with depression who found it an additional burden when their mother told them they couldn't be happy unless they (their teenage son or daughter) were happy. Having a child may make you extremely happy and content, but perhaps it's best to not use that possibility as the sole purpose for choosing to raise a family.

Parenthood myth 5: Having a child will improve my relationship with my own parents

There was a time when it was expected of each generation to pass on the family name and continue the blood line. It was an important aspect of ensuring businesses succeeded and were passed on through the family. Becoming a parent was sometimes viewed as a kind of initiation rite and a way of becoming an adult. I have even heard people state this belief out loud in recent years.

For a woman, providing your family with a child used to be seen as your main purpose in life. Life in the Western world has changed dramatically since those days though and it isn't frowned upon for a woman to get an education and/or to have a career of her own anymore.

Still, old habits and ideals can die hard and sometimes you

will find wannabe grandparents questioning their children on when they can hope to see the next generation being born. The reasons behind their hopes are often connected with wanting to experience the joy that comes from having young children in their life again – and for the grandparents, they can pass these ones back at the end of the day.

There is some truth in this myth for many people; that by becoming parents themselves they can understand their parents' past actions. Empathy with their parents develops from also walking the parental life path. However, unless your parents will be the ones raising your children for you, then remind them that it is a decision that you need to make for yourself. If your parents want to hear the 'pitter-patter' of small feet, they could always connect in with other families with children or volunteer to baby-sit in their neighborhood. In addition, empathy and understanding with your parents can also be developed through honest conversations about their experience.

Parenthood myth 6: Having a child will make my life exciting

Yes, your life will have a lot more going on in it and you will be busier. But some parents say they would rather do the housework than care for their children and others find the baby and child-focused world extremely boring and can't wait to get back to their job.

Also any truth to this myth will depend on what you find exciting in the first place. If you think your life isn't exciting enough, you could consider regular adventure holidays instead!

Parenthood myth 7: Raising a family means I can leave my job

If you are unhappy with your job or lacking a clear career path, the idea of leaving the workforce to raise a family may be tempting. However, many of my friends even with only one child reveal that they don't feel they have this option because both their and their partner's incomes are needed. In families with children, more than half have two working parents.

There are additional problems that can arise from this situation as well even if you can afford to stay at home. Firstly having the pressure to earn resting solely on one partner can feel like a burden for the bread-winner. The person staying at home can also feel trapped or unequal because they are not contributing financially. And finally, leaving work for a long period of time can be incredibly detrimental – the extent of which is fully realized when trying to get back into the workforce when your child leaves home. In addition, parents returning to the workforce after time-out raising children often find that technology has advanced in their old job making their knowledge obsolete (or creating a need to retrain). The old adage 'It's easier to get a job when you already have a job' holds a lot of truth, with potential employers considering gaps in the resume as a negative.

Parenthood myth 8: Raising a family is a good solution to my partner's boredom and a way to make them happy

Having a baby and raising a family isn't a craft project and shouldn't be treated as one. While raising a family is a guaranteed way to feel busier and have a lot more to do, it's way too serious an undertaking to embark on for those purposes.

There's a German saying "Leben durch andere" (living through others) that refers to those who base their happiness on their ability to make others happy. This is a trap I've seen many mothers fall into – living vicariously through their children. To do this means your happiness becomes dependent on others' happiness as well as their appreciation and acceptance of all that you have done and sacrificed for them.

If your partner is already unsatisfied by life, refocusing all of their attention on a baby while neglecting themselves is only going to lead to issues further down the track. Dedicated parents who have lived in this way can end up feeling unappreciated and not accepted when their child grows wings and wants to live a life of their own.

Rather than bringing a new life into the world to curb your partner's dissatisfaction with life, help them find a hobby, connect in with the community, start a business or put some effort into changing your lifestyle together to one that will satisfy you both. Maximizing options for creating happiness is a great idea regardless of whether you'll become a parent or not.

Parenthood myth 9: Having a child will make it easy to fit in with the community or friends with kids

Again, this is one of those arguments that might have an element of truth to it, but is just a shocking reason to bring a human being into this world. I hope no-one seriously thinks its a good idea to have a kid just so they can fit in with others. Just because your friends are having children doesn't mean you can't still enjoy time with them and adapt how you connect with them as new parents. You can create and strengthen friendship bonds by showing interest in their experiences as parents. People with children generally appreciate friends who adapt to the changing situation, and still make an effort to nourish the friendship.

Parenthood myth 10: Feeling stressed about running out of time to start a family means I must subconsciously want kids

Some people panic with the age thing. But you have to ask yourself, do you really want a baby because you want a baby? Or do you want a baby because you fear that you might miss out otherwise?

You might know the fear of missing out if you've ever dieted. The moment you decide to turn something, say chocolate, into a forbidden food is the moment when suddenly your mind becomes absorbed on how badly you want chocolate right? (or pizza, bread, cheese or whatever else it was that you might tell yourself you can't have).

The brain just works this way. Deny yourself something and notice how easily the desire for that item grows.

If you're in the situation of being at an age where you feel time is no longer on your side or you have had some tests done which show the likelihood of getting pregnant is much lower than you originally thought, be very aware of this effect on the mind and check that your reasons for wanting a child do not lie *solely* in the fact that you fear missing out. To go down the parenting path, I recommend having *much* more of a reason than that.

4. DEBUNKING THE MYTHS OF BEING CHILDFREE

It's not just family life that is rife with myths that are good to question. There are also many myths about the supposed carefree life of the childfree. I encourage you to examine the following assumptions and beliefs about how your life will be if you choose to not become a parent. Again, I'm not saying that the following cannot happen. Just, that it is good to not assume, and to make a decision with your eyes (and mind) wide open.

Childfree myth 1: Staying childfree means I'll get more sex

It's no secret that many parents find it hard to maintain the level of intimacy they had before having children. Many primary caregivers also report that sex is the last thing on their mind after a busy day looking after the kids (and often working as well). It's no myth that many parents are feeling really tired and can lose interest in sex at times. Feelings of being unappreciated by your partner and overloaded by responsibilities can also lead to a lowered libido.

But this isn't a problem restricted to parents only. I have talked to many adults without children who also feel unsatisfied with their sex life (due to quality or quantity or both). The key is to prioritize sex and intimacy as well as growth and excitement in the relationship. Otherwise anyone's sex life can dry up.

Childfree myth 2: By not becoming a parent, I'll keep my independence and freedom

Some people find just starting full-time work a slap in the face after their school years or study and the further loss of freedom resulting from the birth of a child can come as an incredible shock. But do the childfree really have more independent and free lives?

Well, it depends on their lifestyle and other relationships in their life. Anyone can find themselves becoming the caregiver for an elderly parent or a sibling. You might feel tied down if you have a demanding job, if you buy a house or lack the finances to be able to travel as much as you wish.

How free or unfree you feel also depends on your personality and your concept of freedom. Some people already feel restricted in a steady relationship however supportive it is and others maintain an inner sense of freedom through the knowledge that they are living the life that they have chosen.

Childfree myth 3: Staying childfree will allow me to travel the world

Most parents will agree that children transform even simple outings such as going to pick up some groceries. Something that used to be a quick 10 minute dash suddenly becomes a much bigger event requiring more time and organization. And it's the same when it comes to overseas travel. Let's be realistic, traveling anywhere without children is easier, quicker, more lightweight and definitely cheaper.

However, when travel is important to someone, they can become very resourceful to ensure they still continue to see the world – even as a parent. From basic hiking and camping trips to house swaps and sharing accommodation with other families to cut costs, there is a range of options to explore. Add in the option of home-schooling, and travel does not need to become a thing of the past just because you are a parent.

Nonetheless, many people find that they have to lower their standards and let go of the idea of traveling as often or as far due to the cost as many parents have less disposable income than the childfree. And as a parent you may also find that your priorities have shifted anyway and what was once important is no longer. You may prefer, for example, to put the money into childcare, insurance or everyday items.

Others discover they continue to travel but have higher requirements of cleanliness and safety than when it was just themselves and a friend or partner, or when traveling alone. I guess you don't find many families in cheap backpackers – but that's not to say you can't find cheap options around the world.

So it is still possible. Travel as a parent will require more thought and energy, but it is possible. Good questions to ask yourself are: What is it that I enjoy about traveling? And can I still create that experience with one or two children accompanying me? Or, does traveling with kids make it more enjoyable than if I were alone or in the company of adults? Might it become more fun to show my child the world and experience the trip through their eyes?

Childfree myth 4: I'll be able to retire early if I don't have any kids

Balancing the budget can be extremely hard for families trying to pay household bills as well as afford things such as school trips and technology items on their child's school stationery list. And with more young adults staying at home longer, that extra money spent is money that isn't being saved for the parent's retirement.

But removing the child or children from the picture isn't all that's required to be able to retire early if that is your goal. You still need a regular, well-paying job or other income source, a retirement plan and good saving habits! I've worked with people without children in their 40s and 50s who were heavily in debt and living week to week with little in the way of savings.

In addition, for some people, 'necessity' is a powerful motivator. With a child to provide for and the desire to be a positive role-model, parents can experience a kick-start in business creativity and ambition that was previously untapped.

Childfree myth 5: My partner will always be there for me (instead of absorbed in raising our child if we had one)

Relationships take time, dedication and effort. Raising a family often requires making even more of an effort to maintain the relationship between you and your partner. But it would be a mistake to imagine that just because you don't have kids, you can rely on your partner to always be there for you. If you want a strong relationship (regardless of your family status) you will have to build and *keep building* your relationship. When you are doing this, then you will be able to reap the benefits.

Childfree myth 6: I'll have a great body if I don't have kids

It's true, being a mum puts extra stress on your body and there will be changes to your body if you go through pregnancy and birth that are much less likely or even very unlikely to happen if you stay childfree. I've also had male friends talk about feeling frustrated with their 'dad-bod'.

Still, I hate to break it to you, but skipping pregnancy and parenthood wont guarantee you abs of steel and toned thighs. But you knew that already, right?

Childfree myth 7: A childfree life is less stressful

Research paints the life of a parent as a roller-coaster with daily ups and downs of moods – from joy to guilt and fear. It is emotionally hard work. In general, there is truth to this myth – if you add a child to your life, you will be dealing with added stress. But, how stressful is your life already?

On the one hand, we could say stress levels in a person's life depend on their job, relationship, home and community, and amount of support received by others, among other factors. The amount of stress experienced as a parent would also depend on the child or children. The first weeks of a newborn's life, for example, can be hell or bliss for its parents purely due to whether the baby is sleeping at night and feeding successfully or not.

But on the other hand, the way we experience the world is not a result of the events themselves, but how we react and deal with them. So, how good are you at dealing with potentially stressful events? Some people need stability and calmness in their life, while others enjoy drama and change. If you want to lower stress in your life, you can learn to do so by changing the way you perceive events – by practicing the ability to step back and find a different perspective on a situation, by learning to support yourself with positive thoughts and beliefs.

Childfree myth 8: Being childfree allows me to have a great career

I would say the argument that staying childfree allows someone to build a solid career is true only if they have dedication and passion for the career they have chosen. Otherwise, you may find that you have all the time to work extra hours, to cover the shifts of your colleagues with children and to take on more and more responsibilities, but will you care about any of this if you hate your job?

Parents around the world manage to build strong careers despite raising a family. As I wrote earlier, sometimes an internal drive is awakened within a parent who wants to succeed and provide for their children. If they want to build a career while also raising a family, then there are many sacrifices that will need to be made (that the childfree don't have to even consider) and for a parent it might be unlikely (depending on the job) that they can also take an extended time out of the work-force to be a stay-at-home-parent. But it can be and has been done.

5. POSITIVE GOALS VS NEGATIVE GOALS

This is something I want you to keep in mind as you continue to think of this topic and your reasons for wanting to raise a family or why you want to remain childfree. When you go through your reasons, I really encourage you to look at whether each of your key reasons is positive or negative. By that I'm referring to the wording and feeling of the reason as well as the 'direction' of the motivation; whether it's 'towards' or 'away from'. And here is what I mean by that:

Take exercising for example. One person might say they want to exercise because they want "to have a strong and healthy body" (this is a towards goal). Another person might also say they want to exercise, but their motivating reason is "to avoid getting fat" (this is an away-from goal). Although both types of motivation can be equally powerful in helping you achieve your goal, negative and 'away from' reasons can feel a lot more stressful because you are constantly focused on what you want to avoid.

Someone once described it to me as the difference between running towards the butterflies vs running away from the tigers. Both are talking about the act of running, but each experience has a completely different feeling to it.

The presence of 'away from' or negative reasons can also alert you to unhelpful and limiting beliefs or unresolved issues from your past. By identifying such beliefs and issues and then working on resolving them, you allow old stress and tension to be released on the topic which frees you up to more easily decide from a more emotionally balanced position.

In addition to the freeing feeling that the clearing of limiting beliefs and emotions can result in, having more positive and 'towards' reasons means that you become focused on what you actually want in life rather than what you don't want. This in itself has its own benefits of giving purpose, clarity and direction instead of just running away from something and stumbling into your unplanned future.

Some examples of 'away from' or negative reasons on the parenting topic (you'll recognize some of these from my earlier chapter on parenthood myths and weak arguments):
– I don't want to become pregnant because I'd never lose the pregnancy weight
– I'm going to have kids because I don't want to be alone
– We're not going to have a child because it'll ruin our relationship

Examples of positive, 'towards' reasons:
– I want to raise a child because I want to teach them all about the world
– I want to remain childfree so I can keep my current

lifestyle which works really well for me
– I decide to have a family because the idea makes me feel really warm inside

I'm not suggesting to ignore any reasons against having children. I'm saying that negative reasons make the decision more confusing because they are their own issues that are probably useful to work on. Doing this allows you to eventually feel more relaxed and sure in life no matter what your decision is in the end.

6. EXERCISES TO HELP YOU DECIDE – PARENTHOOD OR CHILDFREE

Now that we've demystified some common beliefs, this section is all about getting personal - because after all, you're reading this book to get help with making a decision that is going to work for you.

At this stage of the book, I'm sure you're still feeling torn between the options. The focus and purpose of the following exercises is to turn that dilemma into a decision that will become clearer the more you think about it.

Remember I have restricted each rating to two opposing options. I know you will often want to answer with a more 'in the middle' answer, but it is precisely the middle, undecided position that I aim to help you get out of – towards a growing clarity for your decision.

Exercise 1: How well do you cope with change and unpredictability?

Life as a parent from day one is all about unpredictability, from a child's health status to their fluctuating moods to the situations they get themselves into. Ask parents with a child/children at any age and they will confirm the never-ending change in routine and unexpected events that keep popping up.

Remember a parent never really stops being a parent – a friend's 40-year-old son needed a place to stay after an unexpected break in his marriage. My friend's wife and he gladly let him stay – he is their son after all. This is just one example, and not every parent would act in this way, but it is a good example of the ongoing unpredictability of the role. Your life will likely continue to be affected by your child whether they are 3 or 30 ... and older.

Think of some times when a situation has been out of your control and you were directly affected. If you can't think of any from your own life right now, then consider your reaction in the following situations:

– A friend changes plans last minute and can no longer meet you for coffee.
– After a week of excited anticipation you arrive at a restaurant to find it fully booked.
– Your car breaks down on the way to work.
– A friend gets sick and needs you to drive her to the hospital in the middle of the night.
– At work, a new software is installed.
– The zipper gets stuck on the pair of pants you want to wear and you need to leave the house in one minute.
– Your partner surprises you with a mystery weekend away.

Considering the situations given and some from your own

life experiences of unexpected change and unpredictability, how flexible are you when it comes to adapting when life requires it of you?

Rate yourself: How well do you cope with change and unpredictability?

A. I'm not at all comfortable with change and typically try to keep everything in my life stable and predictable.

B. I enjoy acting spontaneously - it makes life interesting. I am generally able to adapt where and when I'm required to.

Exercise 2: Life enjoyment – How important are elements of your childfree existence? (as an individual and/or as a couple)

Until your baby is old enough to be in care of some sort, you will probably find you have little if any 'me' time unless you live in a community with lots of support from family and friends or can afford a child-minder. Most of your time alone or while your child is sleeping, you may be busy completing chores or falling into bed yourself or going to work. Of course this changes dramatically from year to year as a child grows. As a newborn, they will require nearly all of your attention. As a baby, most of it. As a toddler, in some ways less and others more as they become mobile and start exploring.

Many mothers talk about the mixed blessing of kindergarten and early school years because they suddenly have some hours free to do work around the house or go to a job (indeed many mothers talk of their work hours as being their 'me time'). Yet spending time apart from their loved one can be very challenging emotionally. You most likely have to get past those initial years where your child is either crawling all over you, wanting hugs and stories, your constant attention and help (none of which are necessarily unpleasant – to the contrary, these can be some of the most cherished memories of a parent) until you can easily spend long periods of time alone or with your partner. The age at which this can happen will also depend a lot on your child's personality and needs.

For this section, consider your day-to-day routine and what makes you feel satisfied with life, then answer the following:

– How important is quiet 'me' time
– How important is 'just the two of us' time

If these questions or even the situation feels like a non-issue for you, that's fine. But if you answered one or both of the above questions as 'very important', you might want to consider what options you have to ensure those needs continue to be met.

Some ideas and solutions that work for parents depending on their living and financial situation:

– For couples, each parent has a 'me' night where they get to go out and do something by themselves or with friends, or one parent gets special time at home with the understanding that they are not to be disturbed.
– Getting a paid or unpaid caregiver in (babysitter vs friend or family member) so you can spend time together as a couple.
– From a certain age on, having an understanding in the house at times that it's quiet time and everyone is expected to self-entertain. (The exact age will depend on the child and your capability to make rules and stick to them).
– Organizing play-dates with friends to allow each other

some childfree time.

Rate yourself: How important is 'me time'?

A. 'Me time' is something I need to structure into my day, without it I don't feel right.

B. Completely unimportant, I feel most comfortable when I continuously have others with me. 'Me time' sounds lonely.

And how important is 'just the two of us' time?

A. It's extremely important for me to be able to have time out from day to day living with my partner to focus 100% on us and our relationship.

B. Completely unimportant. We already don't see that much of each other every day and I'm okay with that.

Exercise 3: Looking into the future

Taking a glance into your imagined future can provide some incredible insights into how your beliefs, hopes and dreams shape who you see yourself becoming. Whether you are consciously aware of it or not, you probably already have some idea of how you imagine your future to be and what kind of person you will be like. You may remember hearing comments by others referring to their imagined futures such as "I'm not going to be like that when I'm old", "I'm going to die a lonely old man", "When I reach retirement, you'll find me curled up next to the fire with a book", or "I'm going to go on cruises after I turn 50."

What about you? When you think of your future 10, 20, 30 years from now, what do you see yourself doing? Who else, if anyone, is also in the picture?

Work out your age in each of these time frames. Most people have some sense of what kind of life they hope to be living in their 30s, 40s, 50s and beyond. What kind of 45-year-old do you see yourself as? What does your day-to-day living look like? Repeat with each of the decades and fully step into your imagined future – seeing yourself, noticing the people you interact with, what you imagine doing for work and for hobbies.

And now check:

– Was a child/children naturally 'belonging' in your imagined future?

– Reflect on the lifestyle you imagined – does that 'fit' with being a parent (keeping in mind that people manage to be parents and live a wide spectrum of lifestyles from isolation in the countryside to traveling the world and home schooling). If you are one of these people who see themselves dying young, then the good news is that parents on average live longer. Why? Researchers tend to find that people become more responsible when they become a parent; they eat healthier, undertake fewer risky activities and generally take better care of themselves. So don't let that stop you.

Rate yourself: Does your imagined future feature a child or children (of your own). Did you see yourself as being a parent. Could you?

A. Not at all. A child would just get in the way and being a parent puts me off course.

B. Yes, at least in some points of my imagined future I see myself raising a child.

Exercise 4: Looking back from the future

What I want you to do in this exercise is to imagine you can time travel out into the future to the point at which you are 80 years old. Once there, imagine you could fully step into this older you and allow yourself to feel your future feelings that come from already having lived the majority of your life – a life in which you were deeply satisfied. See the world and your life's story through your older self's eyes.

– As you look back in time, what are the things that you are most proud of doing, achieving, seeing, and being?
– As you drift over your past 80 years, does it appear that children and/or grandchildren were a part of your life?

Therefore with the insight your 80-year-old self gave you, which of the following are you when it comes to looking back and checking which feels like the harder regret to live with:

Rate yourself according to the absence or presence of parenthood:

A. Looking back in time, I definitely didn't see myself having raised a child/children or having grandchildren

B. When I saw my life from the future as an 80-year-old, I imagined myself having had at least one child.

Exercise 5: Considering levels of regret

This exercise is about comparing two realities and identifying the feelings that accompany each. Connect back in with your 80-year-old self again, as you did in the previous exercise.

Imagine being that age, looking back over a life in which you did not become a parent (or raise a child). Imagine the life you led and notice how it feels to have remained childfree. How much (if any) regret do you feel about having chosen that path? Do you feel a strong absence of having missed out, is there a fleeting feeling of regret that passes because you know you made the right decision, or does it feel positive and absent of regret?

Now consider the opposite: that you are looking back on a life in which you did become a parent (or raise a child). Consider that life-path and the things you had to let go of because of being a parent. Also notice the things you gained. How does that feel in terms of regret? Is there a feeling of regret with the thought that raising a child was at the expense of other opportunities? Or do any sacrifices you made as a parent feel worth it?

The question here is, how much regret did you have imagining that you did or did not become a parent?

And perhaps more importantly, which do you think you would regret more? Deciding not to have a child and then regretting it later in life? Or deciding to have a child and then regretting that you did? Which feels like the harder burden to carry?

The reason why I ask which feels like the harder burden to carry is that there is a high chance that you will regret your decision at times no matter what you decide. A really significant fact about the future is that it's really common for people to wonder about 'what if's', to see their past through rose-tinted glasses as a much easier time and question if they made the right decisions in life.

Rate yourself: Regret:

A. To live with the regret of having had a child feels like a much heavier burden.

B. Regretting that I didn't have a child in my lifetime has a much heavier feel to it for me.

Exercise 6: What if ...

All of this conscious weighing up of the pros and cons that you've likely been doing ever since you started wondering about the child decision can feel exhausting. As I mentioned in the introduction to this book, having a choice in the matter is a wonderful thing (don't ever get me wrong on that), but when it seems that the majority of babies get born as an 'accident', being in the position of having to make a rational decision about this can over time seem near impossible when neither option feels obviously right for you.

I've heard of people on both sides of the fence say they felt a sense of relief when they no longer had to decide. One, when she consciously realized time had flown and she was past her natural child rearing years. Another friend, when after a number of years of to and fro-ing on the topic, accidentally got pregnant after thinking she couldn't conceive. So this exercise is all about the insight you get, when the choice feels like it is taken away from you.

Imagine that you miss your period (or your partner does). Imagine going to buy a pregnancy test several weeks later. See the test device in your hand as you sit on the toilet, watching the little window for the result to show. Now imagine it showing a positive result. Upon seeing this, what happens emotionally inside you?

As you imagined the above scenario did you already feel a kind of excitement as you imagined purchasing it from the store? Did you start having imaginary conversations of telling your partner the good news? Did you imagine hoping for the result to be positive?

Or …

Did your heart drop already with the idea of missing a period? Did you feel yourself wishing the result was a clear negative? Did you imagine being upset, or even considering whether you could go through with an abortion?

Or a mix of both?

And if you are reading this as a partner of someone able to get pregnant: When thinking of your partner pregnant does it make you feel warm, protective, excited, proud and close? Or not right, scared, disgusted in any way, and wanting to turn back the clock? Or a mix of both?

Rate yourself: How did you feel imagining this scenario?

A. What a horrible situation to imagine myself in! I imagine feeling more negative than positive.

B. It felt mostly like something I could accept even though it wasn't planned. I was even excited.

Exercise 7: The unknown chapter

When people imagine having a baby, typically what comes to mind is a healthy child that for the most part gets along with them as they grow up. However, the reality as we know it, simply from looking around us at the people in this world, is one of much more diversity.

If you do decide to procreate, you have no idea what kind of baby you will have, or what kind of child or what kind of teenager or what kind of adult they will be. You don't know whether they will be healthy, be born with a disability, have a serious accident at any stage of their life, become a drug addict, become your best friend, start a family business with you, be a source of joy or heartbreak. All of the details of personality, health and ambitions are not something you get to choose.

In addition, you don't know for sure how becoming a parent is going to change you and you don't know how the experience will change your partner either. There is no way to foresee how you will think differently of your partner and how being parents will change your relationship. All of this is unknown and unpredictable. All that can be guaranteed is change – your life will change, you and your partner will both change as people and your relationship will change, too.

A couple of years ago, I read a comment someone had posted on a parenting blog in reference to the question "How can you tell if you are ready to have kids?" All sorts of opinions and ideas were being added ranging from the absurd to academic. None of which I was finding particularly useful because the comments so strongly reflected the writers' own parenting experiences. That is until I came across the reply which basically pointed out that we cannot see what our future holds and therefore the only question we can ask ourselves is this:

"Are you ready for Chapter 2 of your life?"

Rate yourself: Are you happy with your life as is, or are you ready for the next chapter?

A. No. I don't like the unknown and I am very comfortable in Chapter 1. There is still more to be experienced here. Or, I am ready for Chapter 2, but that next stage in my life could entail change and new developments in other areas of my life; it doesn't have to be a baby.

B. Yes, I feel ready to jump into another stage of life. I'm up for the challenge and feel confident I would be able to get through whatever life serves me. Having a baby could be part of that.

Exercise 8: Reactions to pregnancies

The following exercise gives you another opportunity to tune in with your current gut reaction. You probably don't have to imagine any pretend scenarios in your head for this exercise as life has probably given you enough to draw on.

You are likely to have had the situation at least once where a friend told you they're pregnant. What is your internal reaction? (It may or may not not be different from what you say out loud). If the pregnant friend told you the news years ago, then I suggest you also go ahead and imagine a friend whose life is in many ways similar to yours telling you the 'great news' today and checking what your current reaction would be.

Another situation in which to check your gut reaction can be upon seeing pregnant women in public or within your wider community.

In these situations are you thinking "Oh god, the poor thing" or "Wow, how fantastic"?

Rate yourself: On hearing a friend is pregnant, my

internal reaction is:

A. I might cringe or be concerned for her. I also feel glad it's not me.

B. Excited for her, interested and maybe even jealous.

Exercise 9: Natural desire

If you're willingly going to invite another person into your life, daily routine and your heart, then a very good question to ask yourself is whether you naturally find yourself drawn to babies and/or children already.

For example, do you find yourself declining to hold any baby handed to you or are you the one reaching out? Do you ever find yourself playing with the kids at a family event or do you wish they would play somewhere else so you didn't have to see or hear them? Do you find children's antics adorable or immature? Do you ever volunteer to look after someone else's child or do you make sure people know you are not available? Do you wish you could bring a friends child home with you or are you glad to see the back of them after your visit?

Think of any situations in which you come into contact with children, babies and families. Is there a natural pull or desire to belong to this group of society or are you happy in your adult-only world? If you don't find yourself in situations where you get to spend time around children, you can check your response with children you see out and about in your community and in shops. Some people for example barely register their presence, while others end up smiling and playing games of peekaboo with babies and children in the supermarket queue.

I want you to take your answer with a grain of salt because I have friends who have told me that they don't like kids in general and never have. But, that they were amazed by their love and never-ending interest in their own child/children ever since they were born. One friend confided he still doesn't care much for his friends' children but loves being with his own.

It's your life, and you're the one having to make your own decision. The funny thing about these friends who tell me they didn't like kids until they had their own is that they all had their children as an accident. Think about it. If they really didn't like kids that much, would they have wanted to go down that route if they had had to consciously decide like you have to?

Rate yourself: How much of a pull do you feel towards babies and/or children?

A. Either neutral, or wanting to run in the other direction.

B. I go out of my way to include them in my life. Or: I crave the presence of a child, children or family in my life in a deeper way, rather than just spending time with the children of others.

Exercise 10: Security and support - How much support do you have in your life?

Even though being a parent can be incredibly awe-inspiring, heart-warming and fulfilling, raising a child also takes a lot of effort. When we go through challenging experiences of any kind, our load is lighter when shared with others.

In this exercise, I simply want you to identify the supports that exist in your life. Who belongs to your network of support? Who are the people you can turn to in times of need?

To identify who is in your support network, start by looking at those most close to you and gradually work your way out to community supports. This way you will end up with a list of people which will include people like partner/s, family, close friends, neighbors you have befriended, local child services and organisations.

As you are thinking through the people who are your supports, I also want you to consider how secure that support is. Living with dependable supports is much more grounding than the sometimes anxiety provoking scenario of not knowing if you can rely on those around you. This also includes looking at the stability of your relationship if you are in one. Your partner is likely to be the person you lean on the most. Will they be there for you when you need them?

Some of you will end up with extremely long lists and have many people who provide support in your life, give you a sense of security and the peace that comes from knowing that you are not going through life alone. However, not everyone has a long list and some will find there is a lack of support at a close level. This can be due to situations such as family estrangement or relocating to another city or country away from friends and family.

For those of you with a shorter list, it is even more useful to take note of the community services available as well as notice that many new parents create strong bonds with others from pregnancy or early parenting groups which continue as a new mutual support group. Even blogs, websites and social media interest groups can provide support for those feeling they could do with more.

Rate yourself: What is the level of support you have in your life and how much would be available for you if you were to have a child?

A. I have few supports and I live an isolated life.

B. I have many avenues from which I feel supported and there are additional supports for families in my area. Or: The lack of support and community in my life wouldn't be an issue for me.

Exercise 11: What are your priorities?

There was a time when I was much younger, when my boyfriend at the time was extremely motivated for us to have children. Despite my loving him, I knew that the timing was not right for me. Aside from feeling too young, which was in itself a deciding factor, I also had firm plans to travel and live overseas alone for a couple of years after studying. This was a plan I had had since my teenage years and one that was non-negotiable.

Recently I talked to a woman with older parents who didn't feel able to have her own children, because she knew her parents were reaching an age where they would start requiring a lot of support and care from her. She couldn't see how she would manage both and had thus decided to remain childfree – for her own wellbeing.

Looking at your future plans is important because starting a family requires a lot of focus and commitment. Going into something this serious only half-hearted isn't really a great idea and can lead to parents holding intense feelings of resentment about having given up on their dreams.

Rate yourself: Where are you in terms of room in your life to dedicate to having a child?

A. I have important plans that a child feels incompatible with and I don't want to shift or change them.

B. A child could fit in with all of my plans – now and in the future.

Exercise 12: Decision making

One of the most beneficial lessons I've learned in life is that we already hold the wisdom within ourselves that is required to resolve any current or future situation. It is true, that accessing this wisdom is not always an easy thing to do by ourselves when we need it most – especially when we have not yet become skilled at doing so.

In this exercise, I'm going to guide you to connect in with a vital key to unlocking the parenthood dilemma you currently face. If you look past all of the details of how this decision will affect you, it becomes plainly obvious that at its core lies the decision-making process in itself.

Therefore, let's now look at how you make decisions. More specifically how you make extremely good decisions. And for this, we are going to reach back into your past.

The first step is to take some time to look over your life and identify times when you had to make a decision and the decision you made was a very good one. I want you to identify some of the times when you reached a place of knowing deeply what you needed to do and then had the courage to act on this knowledge and wisdom. There are many times when you would have made good decisions and these will have come in the shape of big and little decisions. Some of these decisions may have felt very hard to make, and some may have even required letting go of something in order to stay true to yourself. Don't judge the content of the decision, just whether it was a good decision.

There is no rating for this exercise. Your only goal here is to identify how it is that you make good decisions. You will have your own unique blueprint for this and taking the time to uncover your successful strategy will allow you to incorporate it into this current decision as well as being available for you to consciously choose in the future for other decisions you need to make.

Write these times on a piece of paper.

Now take some time to consider each decision in isolation. Ask yourself the following:

– Once you knew you had to make a decision, what was the process you went through to find the answer of what to do?
– Did it require a lot of quiet contemplation?
– Did you consult with others? If so, who?
– How, if at all, did they assist you (what did they provide in the process)?
– How long did it take for you to reach your final decision?
– Once you made the decision, how did you 'receive' the wisdom from yourself of what was right to do?
– Did you suddenly find yourself thinking a certain thought which told you how to act?
– Was it a feeling from the heart?
– Did the message come from a gut reaction of knowing what was important to you?
– Was it, perhaps, a combination of head, heart and gut knowledge?
– And when you had that final eureka moment, how did you recognize you'd come to the right decision for you?

Once you have identified the process you go through in making good decisions, you can go through the same steps and apply it to the decision of whether to become a parent. Your personal decision-making strategy will be unique to you , so the more familiar you are with it, the more you can apply it to this as well as other areas in your life.

If you find this exercise difficult to do alone, you may find having someone to discuss the questions and answers with more helpful and revealing.

Exercise 13: Body acceptance

Aside from the obvious pregnant belly that you know you are going to get if you decide to carry a pregnancy, there are many changes that can occur in a female's body because of pregnancy and childbirth, some of which are temporary or treatable, while others you may have to live with for the rest of your life.

If you need a list of options then here are just some of the possible experiences:

– Stretch marks on breasts, tummy, hips, buttocks and arms that may or may not be permanent
– Scarring if you have a caesarian or episiotomy
– Pigmentation patches on your face and/or neck (cholasma aka the 'mask of pregnancy') that either disappear or remain post pregnancy
– A line down the middle of your abdomen (linea nigra) which typically disappears but can be permanent for some women
– Hemorrhoids are common during pregnancy. They may

get worse with each subsequent pregnancy and may never go away
– Loose skin on the tummy which can be hard to shift despite eating healthily and exercising
– Varicose veins
– Changes in your breasts (after all has passed, breasts may end up larger or smaller or with ptosis aka sagginess), temporary darkening and enlargement of nipples and areola during pregnancy and breast feeding
– Fibromyalgia – if you are genetically disposed towards this, it can be triggered by childbirth
– Issues with incontinence (bring on the pelvic floor exercises)
– Sex can feel different or even uncomfortable post birth

The question here is: How secure are you in the acceptance of your body? Can you cope with the changes your body will go through? (If body acceptance is a big issue for you, then you may want to look at working on this in therapy as age will change all of us over time whether we have kids or not!) In addition, can you trust that you would be honest with health professionals and seek help if you needed follow-up physical health care or therapy if you weren't happy with your health or well-being?

Rate yourself on your body acceptance:

A. I already have issues with accepting my body the way it is now.

B. I'm pretty accepting of my body. I do what I can to help myself feel good in my skin and what I cannot change, I accept.

If your partner would be the one having the baby, how accepting are you that her body will change? How much does the way your partner looks affect things like desire and attraction for you? Would it be a game changer? How accepting are you of the changes her body will go through?

Your rating as the partner:

A. The way she looks is very important to me and the way I feel about her. I'm not sure I would be okay with her being pregnant, her breast-feeding or with any long term changes in her body after birth.

B. I truly feel that my love for my partner goes way beyond skin deep. Any changes would be a reflection of the beautiful baby that would be a product of our love.

Exercise 14: Life values: What is important to you?

We each have things that we value in life. I'm not talking about objects like a designer handbag or a car. When we talk about values, we're talking about wider ideas of what is important to us. For example, do you value loving friends or financial security or freedom? Or all three? Other values people might come up with when doing this exercise could be things like: living close to nature, family, having a clear vision for the future, travel, fun and laughter. Your values are what enrich your life and give it meaning. To have them fulfilled leads to increased contentment in life. To have them denied, leads to dissatisfaction. That is why considering them in the contemplation of whether to become a parent is vital.

So considering your life, ask yourself the question "What is important to me in life?" Write a list of everything that comes to mind and then arrange each value in order of importance with the most important at the top and the not as important ones at the bottom. To do this easily, cut out small squares of paper (or use sticky notes) and write each value on its own piece. That way you can easily move them around when figuring out their order.

To help work out the order of your values, you may find it useful to compare one against another, e.g. "Is community more important than overseas travel or is overseas travel more important than community?"

Once you have completely ordered your list, consider how well (or not) your life values fit in with raising a child, and the role of a parent. Do you have any values that having a child would clash with (e.g. peace & quiet) and, conversely, are there any values that are met by the addition of a child? (e.g. ongoing learning). It's up to you to decide whether you believe there is a clash or a fit and this will depend on what you mean by each value in its application within your life. Important: Pay most attention to how well your highest values sit with being a parent.

Consider your discoveries and insights into your values.

Rate yourself according to the fit or clash with the life of a parent and the raising of a child:

A. I believe there is mostly a clash between what I value in life and life as a parent.

B Having a child and being a parent mostly fits in well with my values. They support each other.

Exercise 15: Family values – What is important to you about family?

Follow the above exercise, but this time focus on the domain of family. You can ask yourself, "How would I like to be as a family?" or what you already value in a family (after all, you are part of one already however close or distant). Both this and the above exercise are also important to do with anyone else who will be raising the child with you. An important conversation to have is around how in line your ideas are with those of your partner!

Some ideas of values are: fun, communication, time together, shared learning, support, sense of belonging and so on. Make sure to come up with your own values (don't just use my ideas) and list them as you did with the life values according to importance.

Then check how comfortable you feel around your ability to create this environment within a family if you were to start your own. It may seem a strange idea to try to associate a rating to this exercise, but what I find is that it helps flush out any personal issues that may be beneficial to address first. For example, imagine someone who regularly works 70 hours a week, but also lists 'time alone with my partner' as top values. To start a family without rethinking their career will likely leave them feeling frustrated and unsatisfied with their decision.

Rate yourself according to your family values:

A. My values for a family mostly feel incompatible with the life I am living (or want to live).

B. This exercise makes me feel good about starting a family now. Or, I now know my family values but don't necessarily need to start a family in order to get my needs met.

Exercise 16: The role of memories

The Baby Dilemma: How to Decide

There can be a lot of fear surrounding the idea that having a child is an irreversible decision. Parenthood is a decision you cannot back-track on. Once a baby is born, you pretty much have your new role as a parent for the rest of your life. (Note: I'm taking it as a given that people don't consciously consider giving up their child to adoption or foster care as an option in the case they change their mind post-birth).

But lets face it, a baby is not like a hamster with a few years life expectancy, or even like the average pet cat that will only live into its teens. It may be an easier decision for many to make if becoming a parent had a shorter timeframe attached to it – Like a challenging new job you accept knowing that it is only contracted for a few years. Becoming a parent is a life-long decision and therefore I think it makes a lot of sense that anyone considering this step in life gives it proper thought and consideration. A baby is not a pet, nor a new job. The rest of your life will be affected by your decision and it makes sense that you give it the weight it deserves.

That said, it is easy to over-do the thinking about having to make the 'right' choice, because the thought of making a lifelong commitment and the resulting fear can become overwhelming. Ask most parents and they will tell you how quickly the time passes, how suddenly their tiny baby became a toddler, within a blink was off for the first day of school, not long after seemed to transform into a more independent teenager and before the parents knew it, became a fully grown adult.

Sometimes the idea of time speeding up has in itself scared me, because I enjoy making my life feel like its long and stretched out. However, there are mental strategies to help with the experience of time – fast or slow, regardless of whether you are a parent or not, so this isn't really anything to worry about. Nonetheless the perception that one's child grows up fast is an interesting and important insight to consider within your decision making.

Another element of this – namely, the fear of making a mistake – is useful to consider in terms of other decisions that you have made in life. Let's play devil's advocate for a moment.

Write a short list of some of the things that you chose in your life that led to negative experiences. Some examples might be:

– A job you accepted where you were bullied or that didn't lead anywhere
– A haircut that didn't suit you and felt like it took forever to grow out
– An unsupportive relationship
– A move to another city
– Leaving home too early ... or too late

However big or small your choices and their impact on your life, now consider the following: What was good about the decision you made, despite the negative element? What did you learn? Who are you glad you met? How did you grow as a person? How did that experience change your life for the better? What positive experiences wouldn't have happened if you had chosen differently?

After pondering each of your experiences in detail with these questions, now ask yourself:

If you could go back in time, would you choose to not have that experience (and live with whatever else would have happened instead?)

I don't know about you, but even when I think about the

worst times in my life, when I have been at my absolute lowest, in retrospect, I still wouldn't wish things any different because it has been precisely because of those times that I have gained strength and courage, learned coping skills that I have for life, realized what is important to me in life, relationships and work, met some of my closest friends (and my husband!), and gained an understanding of what goals I want to achieve.

Rate yourself: How easily can you appreciate the good that comes with the bad?

A. I find it hard to see a positive from the challenging times in my life – especially situations that happened because of the choices I made. When I think of those times, I would wipe them from my past if I could.

B. Everything happens to me for a reason. There is something good to be found in nearly every situation.

Exercise 17: Age – How old are you?

This is a tricky question when applied to the family topic, especially for a woman, because it can create panic and women can be very good at imagining the ticking of some kind of internal, ominous clock. Now that's a sure way to get anxious about it!

There are nonetheless many reasons why it can be useful to consider your age and the age of your partner when it comes to beginning a family and for some people it is a deciding factor for them.

Aside from the fact that the older a woman is, the fewer eggs remain in her body, there are many aspects to the question of age. Consider the following:

– If you were to raise a family, do you have a particular age that you see yourself as? If you want to be a young parent, is there an age by which you want to have decided by? For some people, being a young parent is important and they have visions that reflect this. Others aren't fussed by the idea of being an older parent. If you became pregnant now, how old will you be by the time your child turns 10? It's also interesting to note that parenthood is often a motivating factor in itself for people to look after their health and keep themselves fit – which might keep them 'younger' as well.

– If you are reaching an age where, statistically, fertility starts to decline, you may wish to get your fertility tested to get a more personal understanding of the chances of becoming pregnant (or if you are male – helping someone become pregnant).

– Pregnancies in women older than 35 are called geriatric pregnancies and carry more risk for both baby and mother. However, women in their late 30s and 40s can still have healthy pregnancies.

– Are you open to options such as adoption, IVF, and surrogacy? These all increase the time-frame for raising a family.

– If you are a male looking at having a child, remember that sperm quality also declines with age.

Rate yourself according to how you feel about your age:

A. I feel either too young or too old to become a parent at the moment.

B. I am at an age that I think is ideal for me to become a parent.

Exercise 18: What makes you, you?

How flexible is your self image? I'm not talking about physical appearances, but your idea about who you are as a person. As a parent, your role changes in life and obviously your day to day living changes too.

Do you have a strong sense of identity and how that translates into your daily living or do you feel more like someone whose identity is really flexible? Obviously the fact that you too were once a child informs us that you are a constantly evolving being. How you think of yourself now is very different than how you saw yourself as a five year old, for example.

That said, for some people even a slight shift or influence from others can feel like a threat to their sense of being able to stay true to themselves.

Rate yourself: How flexible is your self-image?

A. The concept I have of 'me' – or my self-identity – is tied in with a particular way of living. If I think of adding a kid to my life, I'm worried that I will struggle to keep being 'me' or living authentically.

B. Who I am has changed and will continue to change throughout my life. The essence of me could flexibly live many different lifestyles – I will still be me.

Exercise 19: Pros and cons - Can I achieve what I

want in another way?

The purpose of this exercise is to help shake up any irrational views that having a child or not results in your life becoming a certain way.

Have you already written a list of the pros and cons of becoming a parent? If you have, then get your list out again. If you haven't or you don't know what I'm talking about, then get a piece of paper and create two columns. On one side, list all the reasons why you think having a child is a good idea. This is your 'pros' list (the list of reasons 'for' having a child). On the other side of the page write the reasons why you think having a child is not a good idea. This is your 'cons' list or 'against' list. As you are creating your two lists, think through the things you believe you will gain and lose in each scenario.

Once you have completed both lists, ask yourself the following:

– Can I satisfy the desires and reasons in the pros list without becoming a parent and having my own child (can I still satisfy them in some other way if I stay childfree)? For example, having something like 'having a child gives me a sense of purpose in my life' on your pros list is something that many would agree can be achieved by doing other things in life that create a sense of purpose. There are many childfree people in the world with a strong sense of purpose in life – this is not a feeling restricted to parents. In contrast, a reason 'for' a child could be 'being a mother' or 'raising my own flesh and blood' and those are much harder to attain without actually becoming a parent.

Now do the same with your cons list. Consider each point and ask yourself: "Can that happen even if I don't have a child?" or "Is staying childfree the only way to solve this?"

(The way you will need to ask the question depends on how you have stated the 'con' on your list).

Here are some examples:

'Lose my time and freedom'. Looking at the first question of "Can that happen even if I don't have a child?" To this, the answer is yes. You could lose your time and freedom through working around the clock and you could also lose it by getting involved in a controlling relationship or becoming ill. The thing you are checking is simply whether the argument listed against having a child is solely restricted to the case where you have a child.

Asking the second question "Is staying childfree the only way to solve it?" The answer here will depend on your sense of time and freedom. But it might be "no". Looking at different ways to do parenting could help you find ways to prioritize and keep these elements in your life. If this point is on your list, you might for example find it insightful and a relief to learn how to parent like the French do, who in general place a lot of emphasis on life balance and a baby fitting in with the parents' life rather than the other way around.

Another example: "Get to keep my figure if I don't have kids." Well, this is an interesting one to consider, too. Firstly, can you lose your figure even if you don't have a child? Absolutely. And secondly, is staying childfree the only way to solve it? No. If being fit and healthy is important to you, like many other parents as well as non-parents, you can choose to live and eat healthily and look after yourself by staying fit.

Rate yourself on your pros and cons:

A. The pros are mostly things I can achieve in other ways

beyond becoming a parent myself and the cons seem both significant and highly connected to raising a child.

B. Most of my pros are only achievable through becoming a parent and my cons are mostly situations that could happen even if I don't have a child (or the cons don't really feel like things that concern me that much anyway).

Exercise 20: Confidence in raising a child

I've often heard parents comment that their baby didn't come with an instruction book and that their experience as parents is a constant case of 'learning by doing'. There are, in fact, many instruction books available on every minute topic of child-raising from how to get a baby to sleep through the night, fostering good manners and emotional intelligence, sex education, to giving a child a sense of autonomy and building self esteem. But the sheer volume of information and often conflicting advice on how best to do things can also become overwhelming and confusing.

Therefore, if being a parent largely consists of 'learning by doing', how confident do you feel about raising a child?

Remember, a huge number of new parents have no idea of what they're getting themselves into and manage fine with a combination of the advice given from professionals, friends and family as well as acting according to natural instincts of what feels right for them and their child.

Also consider the lessons you learned about parenting from your own parents. What do you feel they did well? What could they have improved on? And importantly, if you don't think they did a very good job, in which ways could you be different without just doing the opposite of them?

If you do become a parent, there will be things your child will think you do wrong anyway, regardless of your parenting style. Therefore, it's useful to make peace with that possibility and focus on doing your best.

Rate yourself: How do you rate your ability to raise a child (and the ability of your partner)?

A. Very low. I wouldn't know where to start. An ideal scenario would be having someone else do the parenting work with me just being around for the fun stuff.

B. I feel confident that I would know what to do and that I'd pick up what I don't know from others. The topic of child raising doesn't disturb me.

Exercise 21: The question of cost

Statistics put the cost of raising a child up to the age of 18 at US$245,000. UK statistics look at the rate of raising a child through to the more realistic age of 21 – because, let's face it, a lot of kids don't leave home on their 18th birthday. The UK average is placed at £222,458. New Zealanders can also expect to pay around $250,000 from birth to 18 years. Every year these figures increase with the cost of living and although there are many ways in which families can cut their spending, the reality is that a child will cost a lot of money.

For many people who are already parents, the question of how much it was going to cost them to have a child didn't seriously enter the conversation – when you're absolutely sure that you want to raise a family, you can convince yourself that you'll find a way to make ends meet even if you're already on a tight budget. At the end of the day, I'm pretty sure you'll agree that the presence of love in a family is much more important than overseas trips or the latest gadgets. For those, however, who aren't 100% sure they want kids, cost can be an element in the decision that is hard to ignore.

Many parents around the world raise their children on a very low income; some do a good job and some don't. Equally, people can be well-off and incompetent as parents ... or well off and wonderful parents. The amount of money you earn doesn't dictate how you will be as a parent, but it will make some aspects easier.

Consider your income and the potential earning power in your chosen career. If you think you currently don't earn enough to raise a child, ask yourself if you're okay with the idea of changing jobs, increasing your hours or taking on another job.

Tied in with the question of cost is also your lifestyle. Are there things you do now that are only possible due to the fact that you are child free? Would there be other ways to do things if required once a child entered the scene? What are you willing to sacrifice?

If you already earn a low income, it's really interesting to look at lifestyle choices and what is important to you. Some people see a life with children as incredibly desirable even if they had to rely on social welfare (which depending on where you live in the world can range from nil to very generous payments). Others hold the view that they only want to have children if they can still maintain their current way of living.

What about you? How would the cost of raising a child affect your current life? What changes do you think you'd have to make and are you okay with making those changes?

Rate yourself in terms of how you feel about the cost of raising a child:

A. The cost of a child is really unacceptable to me. It makes me feel like it's not really an option. At least for now.

B. The cost is high, but I could always choose to do and give more or less than the average. I'd find a way to make it work.

7. YOUR RESULTS

Now it's crunch time! Time to look at all your results and see what they mean.

You scored mostly A's

Your answers indicate that you are leaning more towards remaining childfree.

You will fall into one of two sub-groups:

1. You have numerous reasons against becoming a parent and feel clearer that you are leaning towards staying childfree for the moment. It could be that the circumstances don't 'fit' in some important ways or that you still have some emotional issues that need resolving before you can become clearer.

Your feelings may change over time, and they may not. You could go through the exercises at a later point and retest yourself, but for now the useful goal could be exploring your own needs and parking the baby question until a later point in time. For now, focus on yourself and building a life of enjoyment and purpose.

Or

2. Through contemplating the various scenarios, you may now feel strengthened in your realization that the life of a parent is not for you. Although you might enjoy spending time with children and might even make a fantastic auntie/uncle/babysitter/mentor, the idea of actually having one or more of your own doesn't seem to be in your future.

If this is the case, congratulations on reaching a decision. You may find it useful to keep your notes and key points on what was crucial in making your decision in case you need to remind yourself sometime in the future.

You scored mostly B's

Your answers indicate that you are leaning more towards creating a life in which you raise children.

You probably fall into one of the following two sub groups:

1. Raising a child feels more appealing and desirable now but you also still feel an element of indecisiveness. In this case, allow yourself more time to ponder your insights and realizations gained through working through this book. Also, continue discussing it with those close to you (including anyone who might be sharing the parenting with you).

Identify if your indecisiveness is due to still searching for the right person to raise a family with or if there are a few key crucial elements that make it not feel like the right move for now. If that's the case, then revisit the exercises when those elements in your life have changed.

Or

2. It seems that having a child of your own would be both enriching and desirable at the moment. Look closely at your individual answers again and over the next weeks and months check what feeling remains. Now it might just be a case of finding out what's stopping you from taking the steps in the direction of becoming a parent?

8. WHERE TO FROM HERE

A couple of years ago, when I started seriously considering whether to have kids or not, a number of friends with children told me that if I should only become a parent if I *really wanted to*. In its absolute simplicity, their advice sums it up perfectly. At the end of the day, they know what it takes and the reality of both how hard and how rewarding parenting can be.

Therefore, after going through all the exercises in this book, and after all the conversations you'll probably have with people with and without children, the real decision is probably going to come from a deep feeling within. After all the thinking and wondering it will just feel like the right thing to do – whatever your decision is. Listen to your rational mind, but also pay attention to what your heart says and what you feel is right for you at a gut level.

When it comes down to the question of whether you personally should become a parent, there are no universal 'arguments' as such for or against – just your own internal wisdom of what feels right – for you. And remember: whether you decide for or against children, you can live a fulfilling life either way.

I hope you have found this book and the exercises in it beneficial in helping you find your way forward in making your decision. I hope you realize that you are not alone in this challenging situation – that there are countless people out there asking themselves the same question.

I would love to hear your, the reader's, journey as you navigate this decision-making process for yourself. I'm also happy for you to contact me with ideas of how I could improve this book. Also, remember that you can give me a review online where you purchased this ebook. I'm sure other people in the same situation will appreciate your honest opinion.

You can get in touch with me by sending an email to maree@nwow.co.nz or you can visit my website to find out more about what I do: www.nwow.co.nz

I wish you all the best in your journey! And I hope that you create and enjoy a wonderfully fulfilling life whatever your decision.

Warm regards,

Maree Stachel-Williamson

9. REFERENCES

Baby Centre. (2014, January). *Will Breastfeeding Change How My Breasts Look*. Retrieved October 19, 2014, from Baby Centre: http://www.babycentre.co.uk/x543044/will-breastfeeding-change-how-my-breasts-look

Bianchi, J. (2013, April 11). *Personal Finance: 4 Dual-Income Households Tell All: How We Save and Spend*. Retrieved October 19, 2014, from Forbes: http://www.forbes.com/sites/learnvest/2013/11/04/4-dual-income-households-tell-all-how-we-save-and-spend/

Curtis, G., & Schuler, J. (2011). *Your Pregnancy TM Week by Week*. Philidelphia, USA: First Da Capo Press.

Defago, N. (2005). *Childfree and Loving It!* London, UK: Fusion Press.

Druckerman, P. (2014). *Bringing Up Bébé: One American Mother Discovers the Wisdom of French Parenting*. USA: Penguin Books.

Fry, E. (n.d.). Oprah Winfrey's Ideas on Choice. Retrieved November 17, 2014, from About Entertainment: http://oprah.about.com/od/oprahquotes/a/quotesonchoice.htm

Gottman, J., & Silver, N. (2012). *What Makes Love Last? How to build trust and avoid betrayal. Secrets from the love lab.* New York, US: Simon & Schuster Paperbacks.

Healthwise, Incorporated. (1995-2014). *Pregnancy After Age 35 - Topic Overview.* Retrieved 10 7, 2014, from WebMD: http://www.webmd.com/baby/tc/pregnancy-after-age-35-topic-overview

Hicken, M. (2014, August 18). *Your Money.* Retrieved October 19, 2014, from CNN Money: http://money.cnn.com/2014/08/18/pf/child-cost

LV Advisor Centre. (2013, January 24). *Cost of raising a child reaches 10-year high of £222,00.* Retrieved October 19, 2014, from LV Adviser Centre: http://www.lv.com/adviser/working-with-lv/news_detail/?articleid=3111218

Lyubomirsky, S. (2014, March 2). *How of Happiness.* Retrieved October 13, 2014, from Psychology Today: http://www.psychologytoday.com/blog/how-happiness/201403/are-parents-happier-or-more-miserable

Ma, J. (n.d.). *25 Famous Women on Childlessness.* Retrieved September 18, 2014, from TheCut: http://nymag.com/thecut/2014/08/25-famous-women-on-childlessness.html accessed on

McGavin, R. (n.d.). *Will your breasts ever be the same.* (American Baby Magazine) Retrieved October 19, 2014, from Parents.com:

http://www.parents.com/pregnancy/my-body/changing/will-your-breasts-ever-be-the-same/

Rodie, C. (2014, September 25). *Motherhood Taboos*. Retrieved October 1, 2014, from Essential Mums: http://www.essentialmums.co.nz/mums-life/10542571/Motherhood-taboos

Stevenson, R. (n.d.). *How Much Do Kids Cost*. Retrieved October 19, 2014, from Stuff: http://www.stuff.co.nz/business/money/5674787/How-much-do-kids-cost

Stone, A. D. (2014). Evaluative and hedonic wellbeing among those with and without children at home. (J. Scheinkman, Ed.) *Proceedings of the National Academy of Sciences of the United States of America, 111*(4), 1328-1333.

The Atlantic. (2014, May). *Do Kids Make Parents Happy After All*. Retrieved October 13, 2014, from The Atlantic: http://www.theatlantic.com/business/archive/2014/05/do-kids-make-parents-happy-after-all/361894/

Thompson, K. (2013, December 14). *A Brief History of Birth Control in the US*. Retrieved October 14, 2014, from Our Bodies Ourselves: http://www.ourbodiesourselves.org/health-info/a-brief-history-of-birth-control/

ABOUT THE AUTHOR

Maree Stachel-Williamson is a therapist who incorporates her own life experiences with professional knowledge from her work and the latest research and experts' perspectives.

Honest and to the point, Maree shares her expertise with the aim of empowering people to find solutions that work for them.

Maree has a diverse training background which includes NLP (Neuro-Linguistic Programming), Person-Centered Counseling, EFT (Emotional Freedom Techniques), Family and Structural Constellation Work, Ericksonian and Clinical Hypnotherapy, Time-Line Therapy ™, Clean Language, Assessing and Treating Sex Issues in Psychotherapy and TFH Kinesiology (Touch for Health).

Other e-books written by Maree available for purchase:

**- Stop Painful Sex: Healing Vaginismus - A Step by Step Guide
- Female Masturbation: Simple Pleasures to Mind-Blowing Orgasms. 2nd Edition.**

www.nwow.co.nz

Printed in Great Britain
by Amazon